HOW TO BE A
LADYBUG

written by **LAURA KNOWLES**

Illustrated by **STEVEN WOOD**

HOW TO BE A
LADYBUG

DK

Hello, I'm Charles Darwing, and I'm in a backyard not very far from where you're sitting now. You've arrived just in time to follow the adventures of a plucky little ladybug as she sets off on life's great journey.

FOR ANY WANNABE LADYBUGS OUT THERE, YOU'RE ABOUT TO DISCOVER:

- WHAT TO EAT
- HOW TO TURN INTO A PUPA
- WAYS TO DEFEND YOURSELF AGAINST ENEMIES
- WHERE TO FIND A COZY SPOT FOR WINTER

If you want to spot ladybugs out in the real world, look out for my **BUG HUNTER TIPS.** They'll give you a helping hand.

Can you spot the ladybug eggs yet? You're going to have to look closer than that.

No, not there. Those are dewdrops.

Nope. Still cold. Those are flowers.

Now you're getting close. Look under those leaves.

BUG-HUNTER TIP

IF YOU'RE LUCKY ENOUGH TO SPOT A LADYBUG LAYING HER EGGS, DON'T DISTURB HER. THE SEVEN-SPOT LADYBUG LAYS AROUND 15–20 YELLOW EGGS, OFTEN ON THE UNDERSIDE OF A LEAF.

Hi, I'm Dotty, what's your name?
I'm Bud!
Hey, I'm Flora.
Oof! That was a tight squeeze.
My name's Marvin... and I'm starvin'!

Boy, am I hungry!
I could eat a horse!
Hey, look over there—APHIDS!
Argh! I told you we should have moved, Brian! Those new neighbors are going to be nothing but trouble!

HOW TO EAT LIKE A LADYBUG LARVA

- DON'T WORRY ABOUT VARIETY. APHIDS ARE YOUR SUPERFOOD!

- WHEN YOU'RE NEWLY HATCHED, JUST SUCK UP THE APHIDS' JUICES.

- AS YOU GROW BIGGER, USE YOUR SHARP MOUTHPARTS TO CHOMP, CHOMP, CHOMP.

- GOBBLE THE OCCASIONAL MITE OR OTHER TINY INSECT IF THEY COME YOUR WAY.

- EAT AT LEAST 10 APHIDS EACH DAY. YOU'VE GOT A LOT OF GROWING TO DO.

Gosh, it's a bit scary down here. There's no one around, not even an aphid. Mmm aphids... Hey, what's that beetle over there? Maybe they'll be my friend.

Hey, stop following me. I don't need a kid hanging around.

Can I hang out with you... Pleeeeease? You look so cool... And I don't know anyone... I don't even know what I am...

well, isn't it obvious? You're a seven-spot ladybug, just like me. Or at least you will be, once you grow up a bit.

I'm going to be like you?! WOW! So, will you be my friend?

Ha, no way. I'm way too busy.

BUG-HUNTER TIP

LOOK OUT FOR LADYBUG LARVAE IN LATE SPRING AND EARLY SUMMER. BECAUSE THEY LOOK SO UNLIKE ADULT LADYBUGS, YOU MAY HAVE ALREADY SEEN THEM WITHOUT REALIZING WHAT THEY WERE.

How am I going to change into a ladybug? I don't look anything like one!
It's so confusing.
Hasn't anyone written a how-to guide yet?

My skin is starting to feel reeeeally tight.

MUNCH
MUNCH
MUNCH

WIGGLE...
JIGGLE...
POP!

MUNCH MUNCH
MUNCH

WIGGLE...
JIGGLE... POP!

18

HOW TO CHANGE INTO A LADYBUG

- EAT LOTS OF APHIDS AND SHED YOUR SKIN THREE TIMES, GROWING BIGGER EACH TIME. THIS WILL TAKE THREE TO SIX WEEKS.

- STICK YOURSELF TO A LEAF AND STOP MOVING.

- SHED YOUR SKIN ONE LAST TIME TO REVEAL A HARD PUPA. STAY INSIDE FOR SEVEN TO TEN DAYS WHILE YOU REBUILD YOUR BODY.

- SQUEEZE OUT OF YOUR PUPA. TA-DA!

Ahh, that was a good snooze...

Hey, you look just like me! Are your wings all soft, too?

Yeah... I just want to be able to fly!

HOW TO TURN RED

- EAT PLENTY OF DELICIOUS APHIDS WHILE YOU ARE A LARVA.

- THIS WILL HELP YOUR BODY MAKE LOTS OF THE COLORING NEEDED TO TURN YOUR WING CASES RED.

- AFTER HATCHING FROM YOUR PUPA, WAIT FOR A FEW DAYS FOR YOUR WING CASES TO HARDEN AND CHANGE COLOR FROM YELLOW TO RED.

- WATCH OUT FOR PREDATORS UNTIL YOU GET YOUR WARNING COLORS. THEY WON'T KNOW THAT YOU TASTE YUCKY!

WHAT IS A LADYBUG?

You'll have noticed by now that ladybug larvae and adults look very different from each other. Imagine looking that different from your parents! Look closely, though, and you'll notice they share some features.

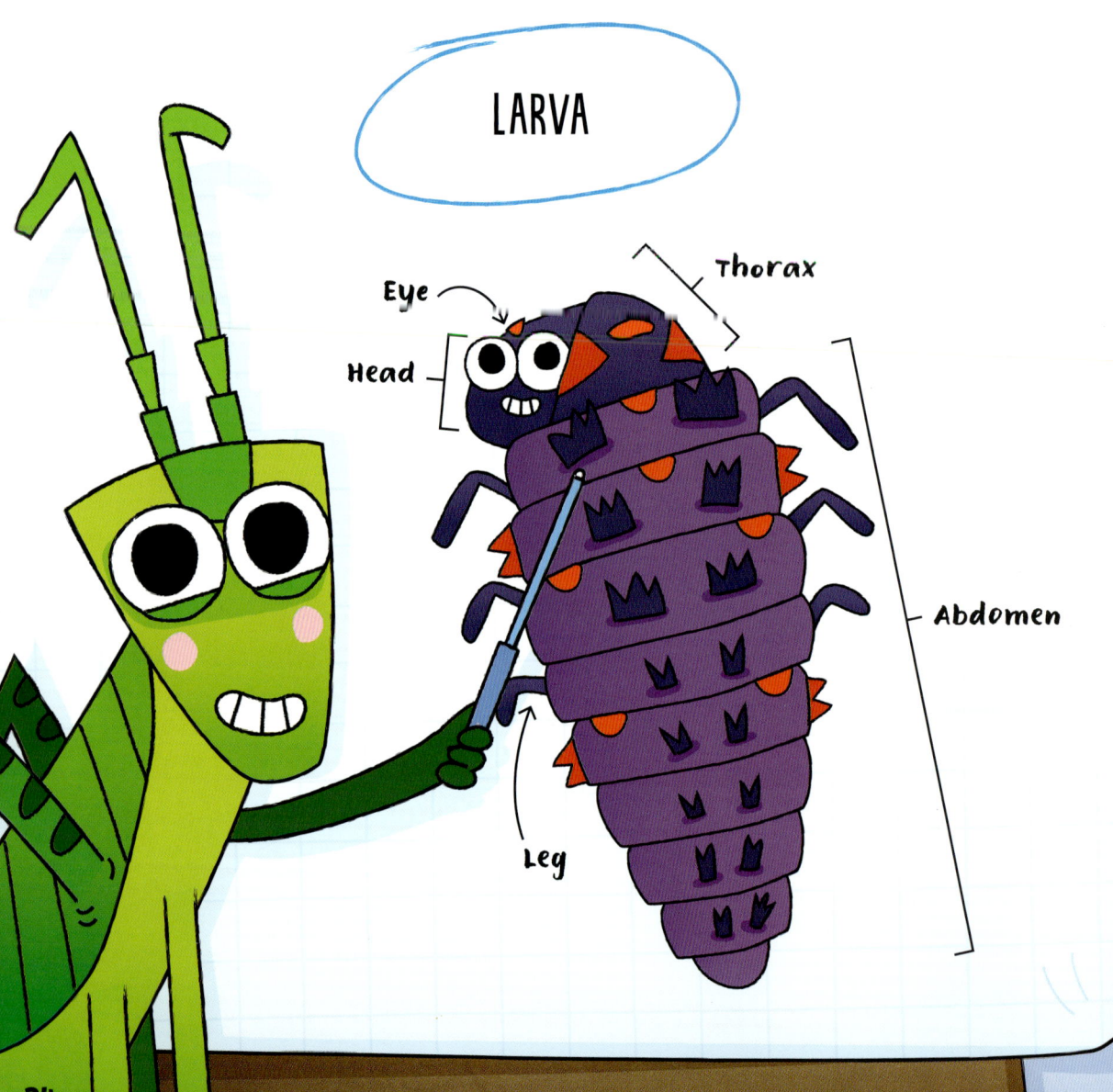

LARVA

Eye

Head

Thorax

Abdomen

Leg

ADULT LADYBUG

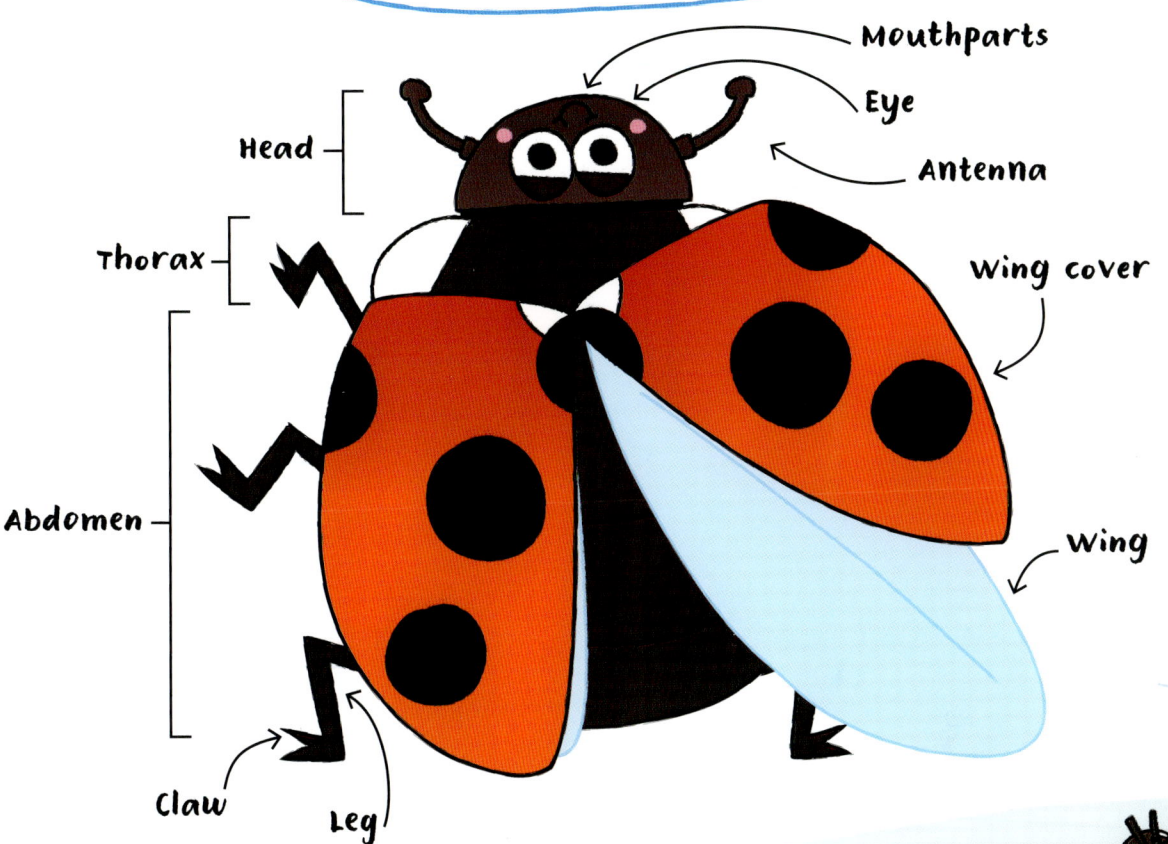

Head

Thorax

Abdomen

Claw

Leg

Mouthparts

Eye

Antenna

Wing cover

Wing

Like all insects, ladybugs have six legs and a body made of three sections—head, thorax, and abdomen.

ELYTRA

THE PROPER NAME FOR A LADYBUG'S SPOTTED WING CASES IS 'ELYTRA' (SAY EL-I-TRA). NEXT TIME YOU SPOT A LADYBUG, SEE IF YOU CAN IMPRESS SOMEONE WITH THIS FANCY WORD.

As our little ladybug waits for her wing cases to harden and her pattern to emerge, she lies low. This is not a time to attract attention. After a few days, her transformation is complete...

YAWN! I've been hanging out on this branch for so long. It's so BORING. I need to get some exercise.

Hold on a minute... MY WINGS ARE WORKING!

Hey, snails! Look at meeeee! Jealous?
Show off.

Snack! Snack! I see a snack!

As you have just witnessed, some birds are not put off by ladybugs' warning colors. While most animals think ladybugs taste revolting, swallows, swifts, and house martins are all happy to gulp down ladybugs without feeling sick.

Nah, too dark.

No, too boring. All the plants look the same!

Too windy!

HOW TO FLY

- LIFT UP YOUR WING CASES (THERE'S A HINGE JUST BEHIND YOUR HEAD).

- UNFOLD YOUR DELICATE WINGS.

- BEAT YOUR WINGS VERY QUICKLY— 85 TIMES EVERY SECOND SHOULD DO THE TRICK!

Ah, this pond looks nice and calm...
Woah, didn't your mother tell you it was rude to stick out your tongue?

Woohoo, a ladybug! Race you!
Haha, you're too slow. I'll catch it!

Welcome to the ladybug Fashion Show! From two spots to 24 spots, there is a pattern for everyone.

Next Up: Eileen the Eyed Ladybug. Tell us: where have you traveled from today, Eileen?

I've come from the pine forest!

Beautiful. Now here comes Velma, a 24-spot Ladybug. Tell us a bit about yourself, Velma.

I don't like aphids! My favorite foods are red campion and false oat grass.

35

Did you know, some 2-spot ladybugs are black with red spots!

2-SPOT LADYBUG
SIZE: 3-6 MM

EATS: APHIDS

HABITAT: ALL, INCLUDING GARDENS AND PARKS

7-SPOT LADYBUG
SIZE: 6-8 MM

EATS: APHIDS

HABITAT: ALL, INCLUDING GARDENS AND PARKS

14-SPOT LADYBUG
SIZE: 4-5 MM

EATS: APHIDS

HABITAT: ALL, INCLUDING GARDENS AND PARKS

ADONIS' LADYBUG
SIZE: 4-5 MM

EATS: APHIDS

HABITAT: WEEDS AND WASTELAND

PINE LADYBUG
SIZE: 3-4.5 MM

EATS: APHIDS AND SCALE INSECTS

HABITAT: PINE TREES

ORANGE LADYBUG
SIZE: 5-6 MM

EATS: MILDEW

HABITAT: WOODLAND

ALL SORTS OF LADYBUGS

There are more than 6,000 ladybug species around the world. Who knows—there might be a few still to be discovered!

16-SPOT LADYBUG

SIZE: 3 MM

EATS: POLLEN, NECTAR, AND FUNGI

HABITAT: GRASSLAND

22-SPOT LADYBUG

SIZE: 3-4 MM

EATS: MILDEW

HABITAT: GARDENS AND GRASSY PLACES

This ladybug looks velvety.

24-SPOT LADYBUG

SIZE: 3-4 MM

EATS: RED CAMPION AND FALSE OAT GRASS

HABITAT: GRASSLAND

HARLEQUIN LADYBUG

SIZE: 8-10 MM

EATS: APHIDS AND OTHER INSECTS INCLUDING LADYBUG EGGS AND LARVAE

HABITAT: ALL, INCLUDING GARDENS AND PARKS

CREAM-SPOT LADYBUG

SIZE: 4-6 MM

EATS: APHIDS

HABITAT: WOODLAND, SHRUBS, AND HEDGES

EYED LADYBUG

SIZE: 8-10 MM

EATS: APHIDS

HABITAT: PINE TREES

They can be many different colors—including red, black, yellow, cream, or even blue! Here are just a few of the six-legged beauties.

The air is growing chilly, the days are getting shorter, and there aren't enough aphids to eat. That can mean only one thing: it's time to sleep through the winter.

Hey, excuse me! It's getting cold around here! Do you know anywhere warm and safe?

You bet I do! I know the perfect old log. All my friends are going to sleep there. Follow me!

BUG-HUNTER TIP

SOME INSECTS AND OTHER ANIMALS SLOW RIGHT DOWN AND STOP MOVING AROUND DURING THE WINTER MONTHS. IF YOU DISCOVER A GROUP OF SLEEPING LADYBUGS IN WINTER, LEAVE THEM AS YOU FOUND THEM.

HOW TO FIND YOUR FRIENDS

WHEN IT'S TIME TO SLEEP THROUGH WINTER, YOU'LL WANT TO FIND OTHER LADYBUGS. TOGETHER, YOUR RED-AND-BLACK WARNING COLORS OFFER EVEN BETTER PROTECTION. SNIFF OUT THE CHEMICAL SIGNALS OTHER LADYBUGS GIVE OFF TO FIND OUT WHERE THEY'RE HIDING.

40

WHERE TO SLEEP IN WINTER

- CRACKS IN OLD LOGS AND TREE BARK
- IN HOLLOW PLANT STEMS
- GAPS BETWEEN ROCKS
- UNDER FALLEN LEAVES
- BACKYARD SHEDS AND OTHER BUILDINGS

Our little ladybug is tucked in, sleeping soundly. She uses very little energy during these dark, frosty months.

zzzzzzz
zzzzzzzz
zzzzzzz

After several months snuggled up quiet and still, the warming weather is waking up the dozing ladybugs.

Our plucky ladybug is off to find some food. Luckily, lots of new aphids hatch out in the spring, making a perfect breakfast buffet.

Aphids... where are you, aphids? I'm coming to find yoooou....

What a beautiful day! The leaves are green, the sun is shining, the birds are chirping. Uh oh! The birds are chirping!

HOW TO STAY SAFE FROM PREDATORS

- TUCK YOUR LEGS IN UNDER YOUR BODY.
- OOZE STINKY YELLOW LIQUID OUT OF YOUR LEG JOINTS (THIS IS CALLED REFLEX BLOOD).
- WAIT FOR THE SCARY PREDATOR TO GO AWAY.
- GO BACK TO MUNCHING ON APHIDS.

LADYBUG PREDATORS

Predators are animals that hunt and eat other animals. Even with their clever defense tactics, ladybugs still have plenty of dastardly predators.

PARASITIC WASPS AND FLIES

SOME WASPS AND FLIES LAY THEIR EGGS INSIDE LADYBUGS. WHEN THEY HATCH, THEY EAT THE LADYBUG FROM THE INSIDE. TALK ABOUT AN UNINVITED GUEST!

FROGS AND TOADS

THESE JUMPY CRITTERS WILL OFTEN GOBBLE LADYBUGS. THEY SNATCH THEM WITH THEIR STICKY TONGUE BEFORE THEY EVEN KNOW WHAT IT IS THEY'RE EATING.

SPIDERS AND INSECTS

SOME SPIDERS, BEETLES, WASPS, ANTS, AND DRAGONFLIES WILL CATCH AND EAT LADYBUGS.

BIRDS

SOME BIRDS, SUCH AS SWIFTS AND SWALLOWS, AREN'T BOTHERED BY LADYBUGS' DEFENSIVE CHEMICALS. THE BIRDS GULP THEM DOWN AS THEY FLY THROUGH THE AIR—ALTHOUGH SOMETIMES THEY SPIT THEM OUT!

OTHER LADYBUGS

IF THERE ISN'T MUCH FOOD AROUND, LADYBUGS WILL EAT OTHER LADYBUG EGGS, LARVAE, AND PUPAE. HARLEQUINS, ORIGINALLY FROM ASIA, PARTICULARLY LOVE A TASTY LADYBUG SNACK.

LADYBUG PREY

Ladybugs are famous for guzzling pesky aphids, but there are plenty of other mouth-watering meals on the menu. Do any of these look tasty to you?

OTHER LADYBUG EGGS AND LARVAE

SOME CALL IT BAD MANNERS. LADYBUGS CALL IT A FREE DINNER.

APHIDS

THESE TINY SAP-SUCKERS ARE LADYBUGS' FAVORITE FOOD.

MITES AND MEALYBUGS

MOST LADYBUGS WON'T TURN THEIR NOSES UP AT THESE MICRO CREEPY-CRAWLIES. IN FACT, ALMOST ANY TINY, SOFT INSECT WILL MAKE A YUMMY LADYBUGS LUNCH.

MILDEW

A FEW TYPES OF LADYBUG ARE VEGETARIAN. THEY EAT PLANTS, MILDEW, AND MOLDS INSTEAD OF OTHER INSECTS.

INSECT EGGS

THESE CAN'T CRAWL AWAY, SO THEY ARE EASY PICKINGS!

POLLEN AND NECTAR

THIS FLORAL FOOD SOUNDS A LOT TASTIER THAN MOLD! ALL ADULT LADYBUGS SNACK ON THESE SWEET TREATS IN EARLY SPRING, WHEN THERE AREN'T MANY APHIDS AROUND.

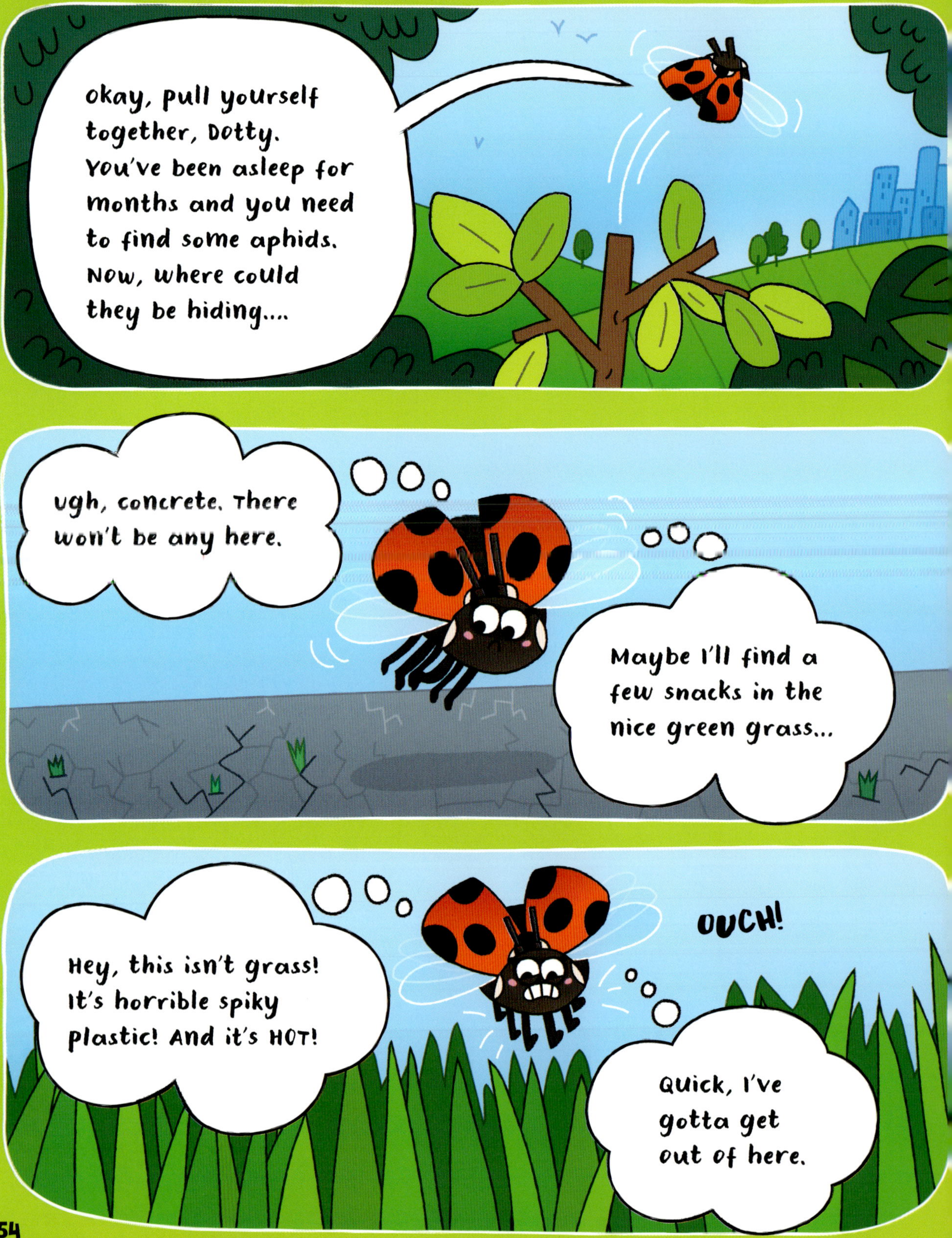

BUG-HUNTER TIP

TO ENCOURAGE LADYBUGS AND OTHER INSECTS TO VISIT YOUR BACKYARD, USE REAL GRASS INSTEAD OF ARTIFICIAL GRASS AND DON'T SPRAY PESTICIDES—IT WILL KILL THE INSECTS.

What am I going to do? Where am I going to go? Is nowhere safe?

Hey, what's the problem? Anything I can do to help?

I've just woken up from my winter sleep and I'm so hungry, but I can't find anywhere safe to land! I can't find any aphids!

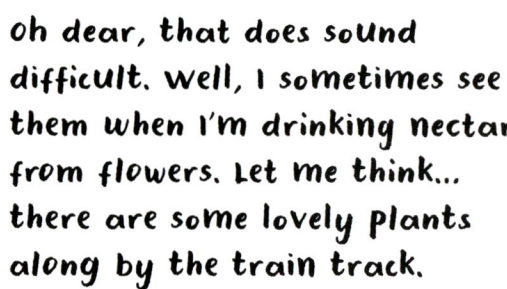

Oh dear, that does sound difficult. Well, I sometimes see them when I'm drinking nectar from flowers. Let me think... there are some lovely plants along by the train track.

HOW TO HELP LADYBUGS

Would you like to make your backyard or balcony an inviting place for ladybugs to live or visit? Here are some simple things you can do to be a friend to these cute and colorful insects.

BUILD A BUG HOTEL

Ask your grown-up to build a bug hotel. Some old wood, pieces of bamboo cane, pine cones, leaves, and a roof of old tiles or short planks of wood will give ladybugs a safe place to spend the winter. Ladybugs also hunker down in hollow stems, so tell your grown-ups not to cut back old plant stems until spring.

DON'T USE PESTICIDES

Encourage your grown-ups not to spray pesticides on their plants. These will kill the aphids that the ladybugs eat, as well as any ladybugs that are on the plants.

GARDENERS LOVE LADYBUGS BECAUSE THEY EAT THE PESTS THAT DAMAGE FRUIT, VEGETABLES, AND FLOWERS.

GIVE THEM DRINKING WATER

Leave a shallow dish of water out so that ladybugs— and other insects and birds—have somewhere to drink when the weather is dry.

GLOSSARY

Dotty's world contains words you might not have come across before. Here you'll find the meanings of some important words to know when learning about ladybugs.

APHID
Sap-sucking bug that is a favorite food of many ladybugs

INSECT
Animal with six legs and a three part-body

LARVA
stage of a ladybug's life after it hatches from an egg and before it becomes a pupa

MOLTING
when a larva sheds its skin

PESTICIDE
Chemical that kills pest insects, but can also harm other insects, such as ladybugs

PREDATOR
Animal that eats other animals

PREY
Animal that is eaten by other animals

PUPA
stage of a ladybug's life before it becomes an adult

REFLEX BLOOD
Liquid produced by ladybugs that puts off predators because of its smell and taste

WARNING COLOR
Animal color that warns predators it tastes unpleasant or could be harmful to eat

WING CASE
Hard wing that protects the more delicate membranous wing

DK | Penguin Random House

Project Editor Kathleen Teece
Project Art Editor Polly Appleton
US Senior Editor Shannon Beatty
Managing Editor Gemma Farr
Managing Art Editor Anna Hall
Production Editor Gillian Reid
Production Controller Magdalena Bojko
Jacket Designer Polly Appleton

Consultant Prof. Helen Roy, Ecologist at the
UK Centre for Ecology & Hydrology and
Professor of Ecology at the University of Exeter

Royal Entomological Society

Director of Publishing Emilie Aimé
Outreach and Engagement Officer Francisca Sconce

Royal Entomological Society – enrich the world
with insect science **www.royensoc.co.uk**

First American Edition, 2025
Published in the United States by DK Publishing,
a division of Penguin Random House LLC
1745 Broadway, 20th Floor, New York, NY 10019

A catalog record for this book
is available from the Library of Congress.
ISBN 978-0-5939-6539-9

DK books are available at special discounts when purchased
in bulk for sales promotions, premiums, fund-raising,
or educational use.
For details, contact: DK Publishing Special Markets,
1745 Broadway, 20th Floor, New York, NY 10019
SpecialSales@dk.com

Printed and bound in China

www.dk.com

MIX
Paper | Supporting
responsible forestry
FSC™ C018179

This book was made with Forest
Stewardship Council™ certified
paper – one small step in DK's
commitment to a sustainable future.
**Learn more at www.dk.com/uk/
information/sustainability**

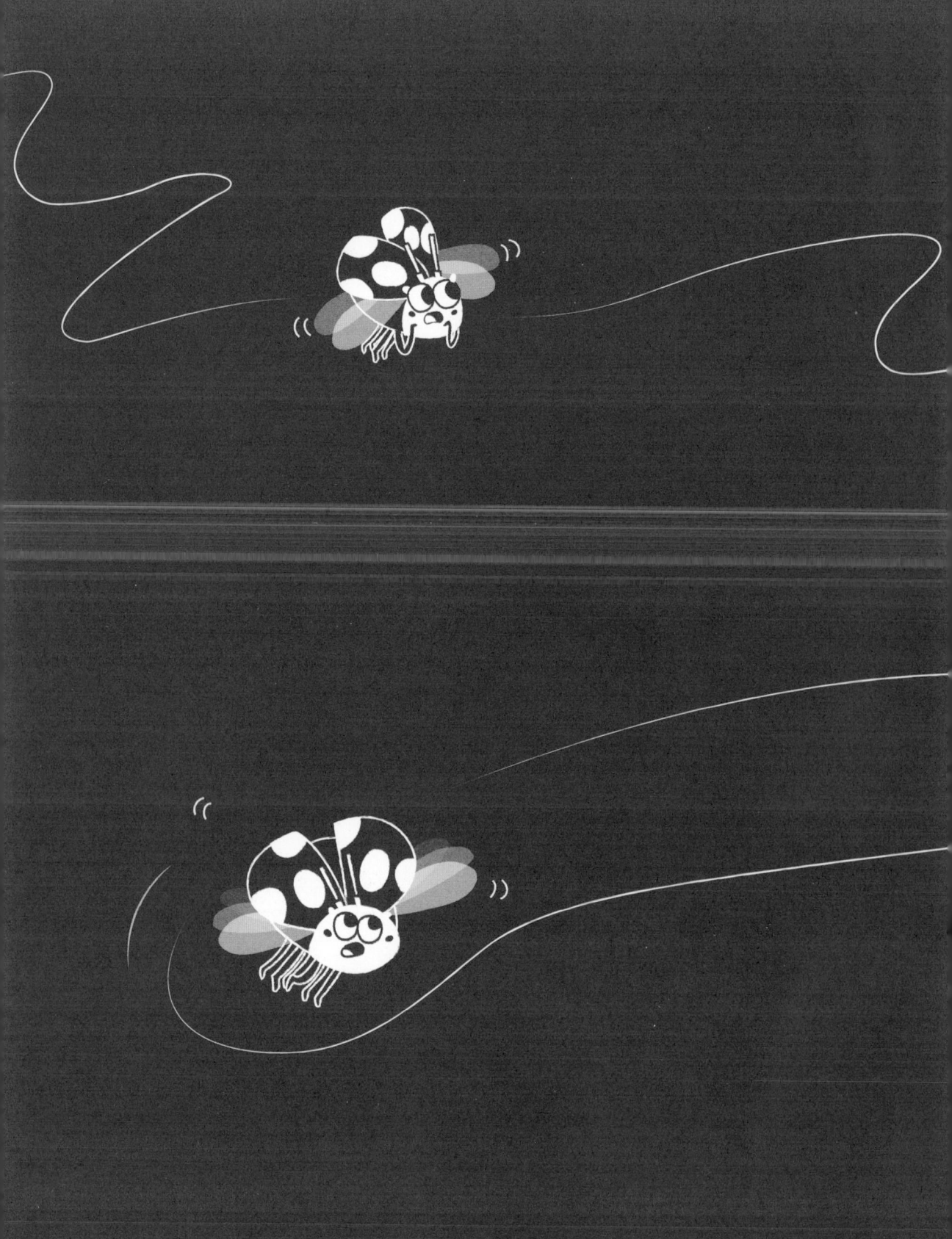